Best Wishes

[signature]

Birmingham the
Black Country
and beyond with
Mac an' 'Im

"E's 'Im... I'm me... but more important... we're us."

It was a chance remark that gave birth to this new book.

"Cuddles" and I were visiting friends at Balsall Common, Sue and Doug Timmis, Doug being an official of "The Jewellery Quarter Association".

Whilst looking at my trilogy of books; "*A Paddle in Hockley Brook*", "*War trickles into Hockley Brook*", and the latest "*An Overflow from Hockley Brook*", Doug remarked about my painting on the covers, and inside. He went on "Ron, you should not keep this talent just to your written books, you should publish a book containing your paintings and cartoons alone". I thanked Doug for this and for sometime afterwards thought about it.

Eventually, after several discussions with "Cuddles" I approached my dear friend Mac Joseph who, incidentally is a very successful author himself of "*Good Morning Ladywood*" fame.

Mac was immediately excited by the idea, and again we had lengthy talks on the matter. The contents are indeed a record of the history of both Birmingham and the Black Country which will retain for the people of both these areas a pictorial reminder of how it was in the Twenties, Thirties, Forties and Fifties and, combined with Mac's books, and mine will give a complete version of those times forever.

Mac for his part has spent so many hours compiling and reproducing my work through one of his technical and talented staff, Jean.

Both Mac and myself owe thanks and a whole lot more to Dr Carl Chinn, Jenny Wilkes, the BBC in general, the Sunday Mercury, Express and Star, Lichfield Post, Lichfield Mercury and Cannock Chronicle for their interest, support, and publicity in what we do for our particular birthplaces, and beyond.

Last, but definitely not least, we assure you, the readers of our volumes, that without you, we could not be us.

If you require separate prints, cards, or books give Mac a ring on 01785 660214 or Smudge on 01543 685319.

Thank you, for being you.

Foreword

Brummagem past leaps into life through the evocative, intuitive and memory-raising drawings of Ron Smith. With a rare skill, he calls back to mind the streets, the buildings, the vehicles and the folk of a way of life that has gone but recently but which today seems lost deep in history. In what is now a visual world, Ron's portrayals of working-class scenes are a vital gift which allow young people to see the childhoods of their moms and dads and nans and grandads.

Yet Ron's power is not just in bringing to the fore the look of Old Brum, it is also in heightening all of the senses in relation to our city's past. When drawing the workers knocking off from Lucas's in Great King Street, he makes us hear once more the factory bull and touch yet again the steel bars on the buses; when he sketches the Scribban's bread van he induces us to taste not only the cottage loaves of yester year but also to smell the horse muck which so many kids scooped up into buckets to sell to those with gardens.

Ron is a man whose work encourages us to use all our senses when we look back. Through bringing into play those senses, he allows us to tell our children and grandchildren about our past in a more sympathetic and effective way.

Dr Carl Chinn

"The Swan"
Yardley
about 1920

The Swan
Coventry Road
Yardley
1920

the junction of
Grove Lane
and
Soho Road
Handsworth
1938.

"Two Birmingham City tramcars"

The top picture depicts the terminus at "The Swan" Yardley, and the bottom picture depicts the junction of Soho Road and Grove Lane, Handsworth, Birmingham 21.

Both pictures are in the year 1938

"Hockley Brook"
Hockley, Birmingham 19. 1938

"Hockley Passenger Station and Goods Yard"
Park Road, Hockley, Birmingham 18. 1936

"Edmund Street, at the junction with Margaret Street"
Birmingham 3. 1938

"Central Fire Station"
Lancaster Place, Birmingham 3. 1949

"Saturday Night Out up the Fanny Brown"
Albert Street, Birmingham 4. 1937

"The Railway Inn"
The junction of Wellington Street, Winson Green, Birmingham 18 and
Vittoria Street, Smethwick, Staffordshire. 1937

"Handsworth Grammar School"
Grove Lane, Handsworth, Birmingham 21. 1936

"Tramcar terminus"
Junction of Byron Road and Waverley Road, Small Heath, Birmingham 10. 1910

"The Turk"
The junction of Hockley Hill and Icknield Street, Hockley, Birmingham 19.
In the thirties

"New Street Railway Station"
Birmingham 2. In the thirties

"Scribban's Bakery"
Lodge Road, Hockley, Birmingham 18. 1938

"Cold Rush"

A Winter scene at the junction of New John Street West and Hockley Hill, Birmingham 19. 1938

"Winter Sunset"

A Winter scene at the junction of Spring Hill and Dudley Road, Birmingham 18. 1936

"The Abbey Vaults"
At the junction of Park Road and Lodge Road, Hockley, Birmingham 18.
In the thirties.
Sold to Mr & Mrs Chris Fent

"The Last Bull of the Day"

Joseph Lucas's Works, Gt King Street, Hockley, Birmingham 19. 1939

"Hockley Passenger Station and Goods Yard"
At the junction of Park Road and Icknield Street, Hockley, Birmingham 18. 1938

"A nice cuppa tea at the bundy clock"
Junction of Well Street and New John Street West, Hockley, Birmingham 19. 1938

"Chamberlain's Clock"

At the junctions of Vyse Street, Warstone Lane and Frederick Street, Hockley, Birmingham 18. In the thirties

"The Old and the New"

The Phasing out of the tramcars, and the introduction of buses.

At the junction of Wellington Street, and Foundry Road, Winson Green, Birmingham 18. 1947

"Swallow Raincoats (Fine in the rain)"

At the junction of Gt Hampton Street and Well Street, Hockley, Birmingham 19. In the thirties

"The Gothic Tavern"

At the junction of Gt. Hampton Street and Gt Hampton Row, Hockley, Birmingham 19.

In the thirties

"Hockley Passenger Station and Goods Yard"
Park Road, All Saints Street, Pitsford Street, Hockley, Birmingham 18.
In the thirties

"Lloyds Bank"
Great Hampton Street, at the junction of Harford Street, Hockley, Birmingham 19.
In the thirties

"Summer Lane Post Office and the only pub that was really in the Lane, The Vine"
Summer Lane at the junction with New John Street West, Hockley, Birmingham 19.
In the thirties.

"The Old Steam Clock"
Morville Street, Ladywood, Birmingham 15.
In the thirties

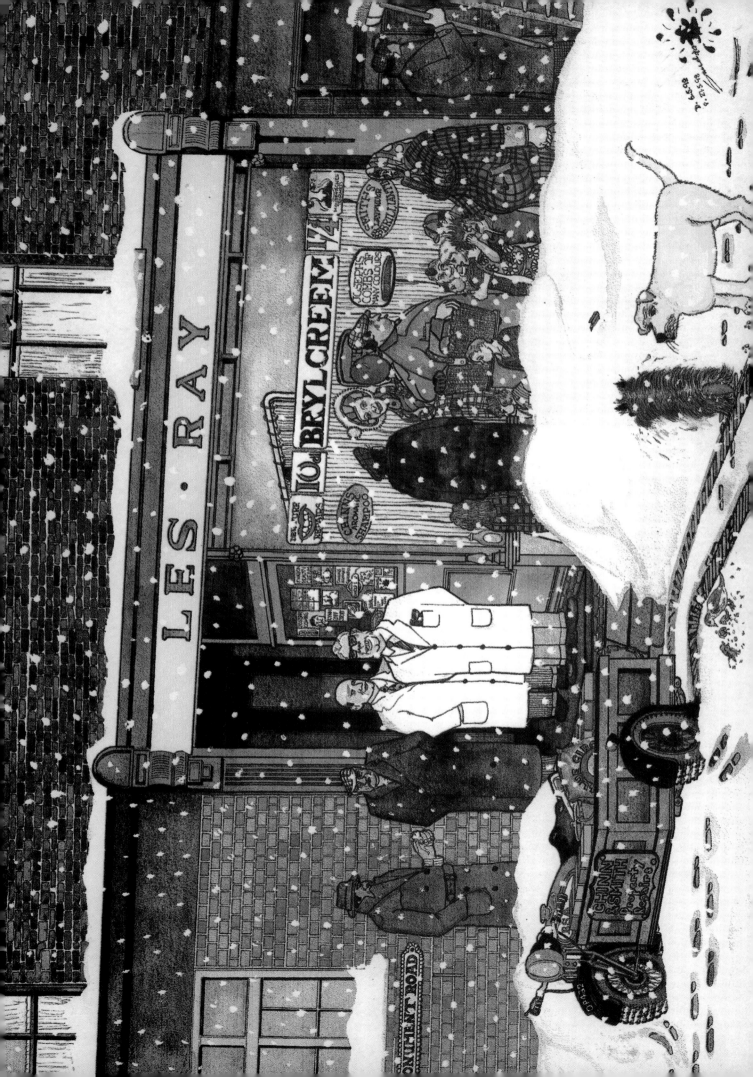

"Les and Ray Joseph's Hairdressers"
375 Monument Road, Ladywood, Birmingham 16.

"Spring Hill Library"
Ladywood, Birmingham 18.
In the thirties

"Good Morning Ladywood"
Monument Road at the junction with Ledsam Street, Ladywood, Birmingham 16.
In the thirties

"A Golden Time"

Handsworth Wood Station, Hamstead Road, Handsworth, Birmingham 20.

In the thirties

"Hockley Tramcar Dept"
Whitmore Street, (The Tram Sheds!) Hockley, Birmingham 19. 1937

"Worthingtons Coaches"
Hurst Street, Birmingham 5

"Coming Home"

"The river Severn"
Bewdley, Worcestershire

"Dartmouth Square"
West Bromwich, Staffordshire.
In the twenties

"Farley's Tower"
Carters Green, West Bromwich, Staffordshire. 1938

"The Stone Cross Inn"
The junction of Walsall Road and Hall Green Road, Stone Cross,
West Bromwich, Staffordshire. About 1920

"The Sandwell Arch"
Birmingham Road, West Bromwich, Staffordshire.
About 1938

"The Annual Sunday School Trip"
Paradise Street Railway Station, West Bromwich, Staffordshire.
In the thirties

"Saturday Evening"
Birmingham Street, looking towards Dudley, Oldbury, Worcestershire. 1938

"The Market Place and the Limerick"
Gt Bridge, Staffordshire.
In the thirties

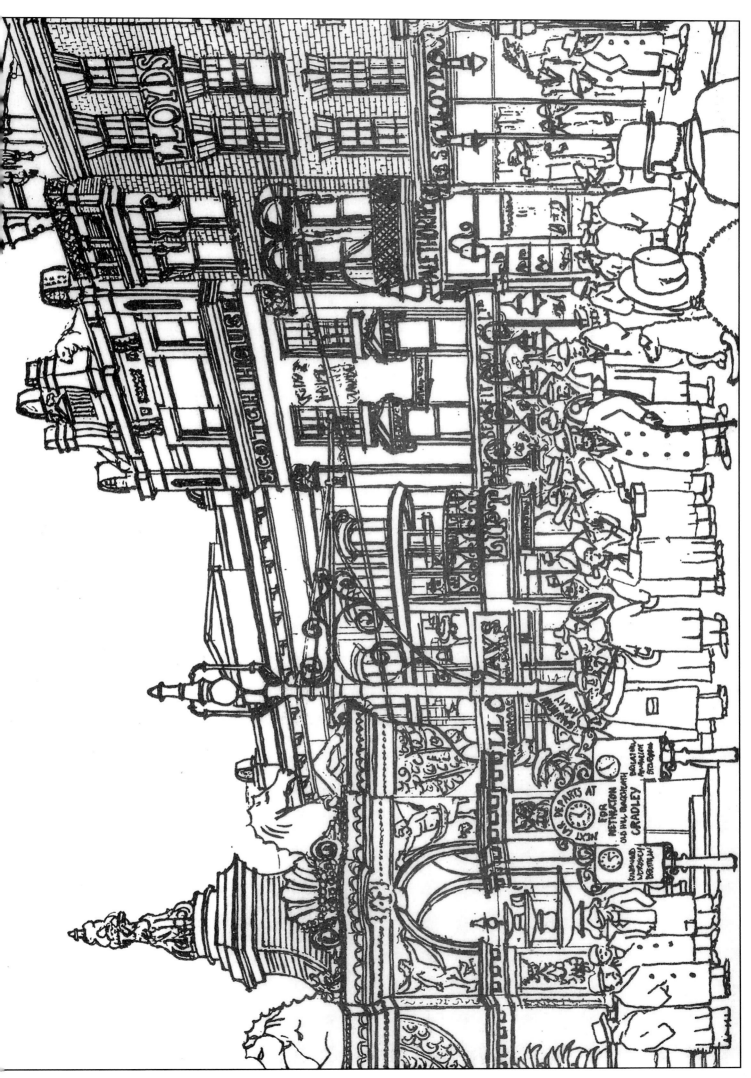

"The Market Place"
Dudley, Worcestershire.
Christmas 1911

"High Street"
Stourbridge, Worcestershire.
About 1910

"Midland Red en route to Birmingham from Burton on Trent". In the thirties.

"Lichfield Cathedral"
From Stowe Pool

"Mrs Cross's General Store"
Little King Street, Hockley, Birmingham 19.
In the thirties

"Our Mom and Dad"

"Our Gran and Grandad"

"2 back of 24 Guest Street"
Hockley, Birmingham 19

"Christmas Eve on the last train home"

"The Manor"

"Winter Sunset"

"The Arrangement"   Savage
                                       98

"Edythe's Christmas Arrangement"

FROM:

86

TO:

" Oswald the Otter "

"Oswald the Otter"

"At the end of the day"

The passage to the Great Western Railway's stables.

The entrance being at the junction of All Saints Street, and Crabtree Road,

Brookfields, Birmingham 18.

In the thirties.

"A stroll up the 'cut' on a Sunday afternoon"

" LEAVE IT TO SMUDGE THEY SAID.
DON'T WORRY THEY SAID. 'E'LL GERRA
COACH FER THE AWAY MATCH AT PRESTON
A-R-R, 'E'S GORRUS A BLOODY COACH
ORIGHT, JUS' LOOK ARRIT. WE'LL BI
THE BLOODY LAUGHIN' STOCK AT DEEPDALE !!. ''

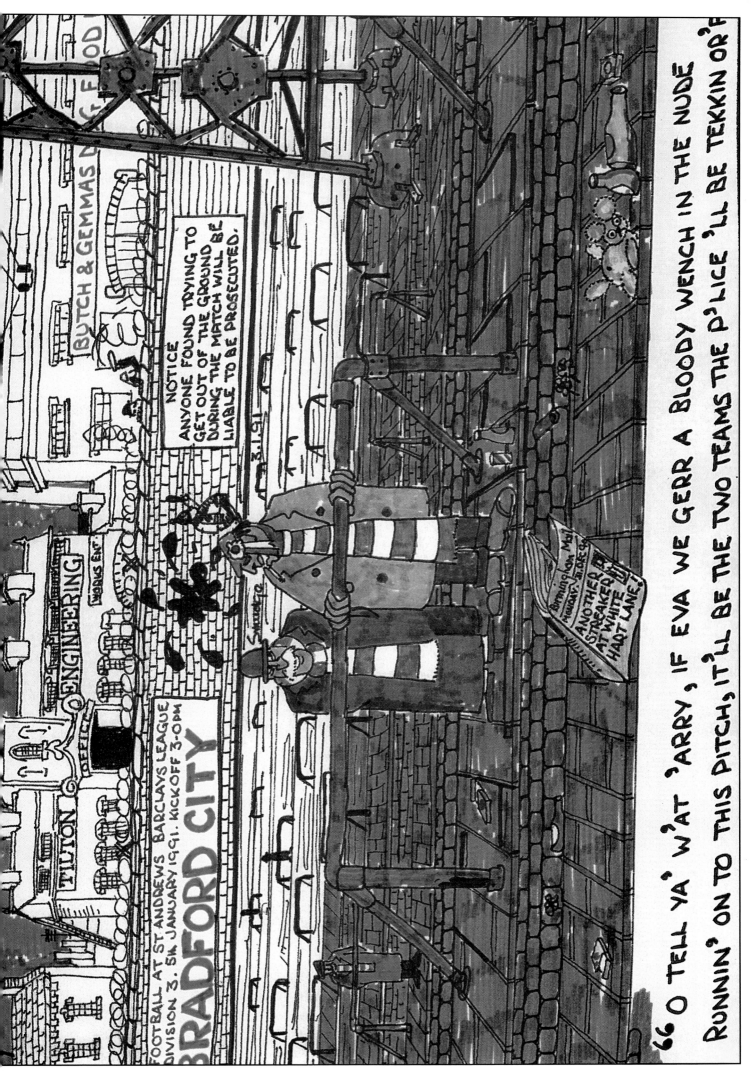

"O TELL YA' W'AT 'ARRY, IF EVA WE GERR A BLOODY WENCH IN THE NUDE RUNNIN' ON TO THIS PITCH, IT'LL BE THE TWO TEAMS THE P'LICE 'LL BE TEKKIN OR!"

To:

"Popeye"

FROM:

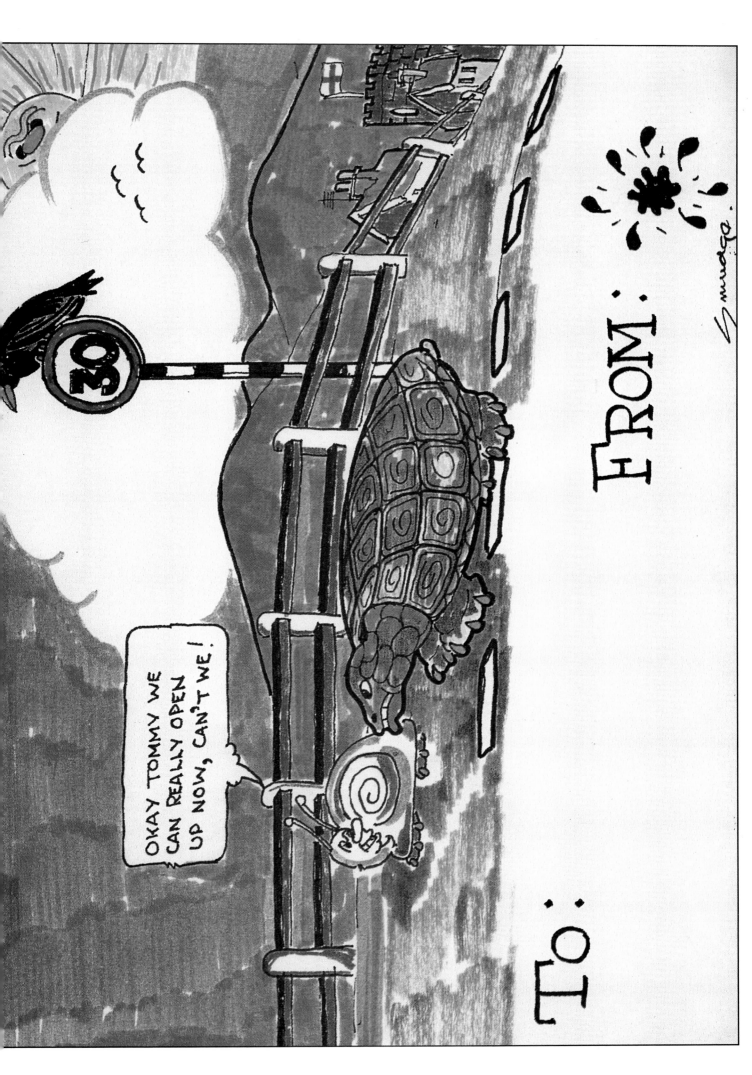

To:

FROM:

BILLY BADGER — THE ROAD WATCHMAN.

Mick and Maud on the Stafford Moor.

" THEIR WILL BE NO CHARGE TODAY " (HE'S HAVING HIS HORN SHARPENED)

You are cordially invited to

THE MUDLARK

AT. THE **HIPPO**DROME

STAFFORD

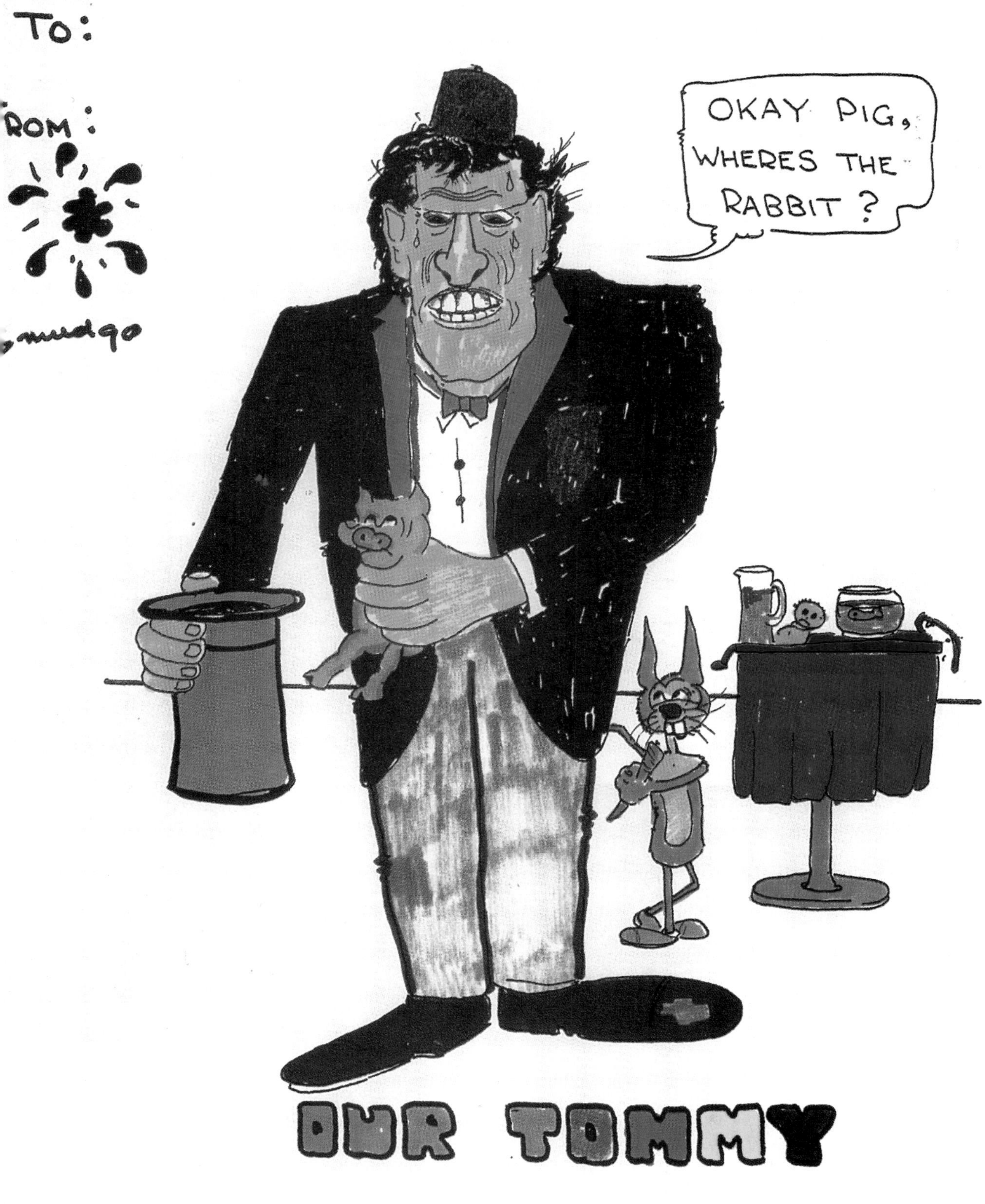
TO:
ROM :
OKAY PIG, WHERES THE RABBIT ?
OUR TOMMY

TO:

FROM:

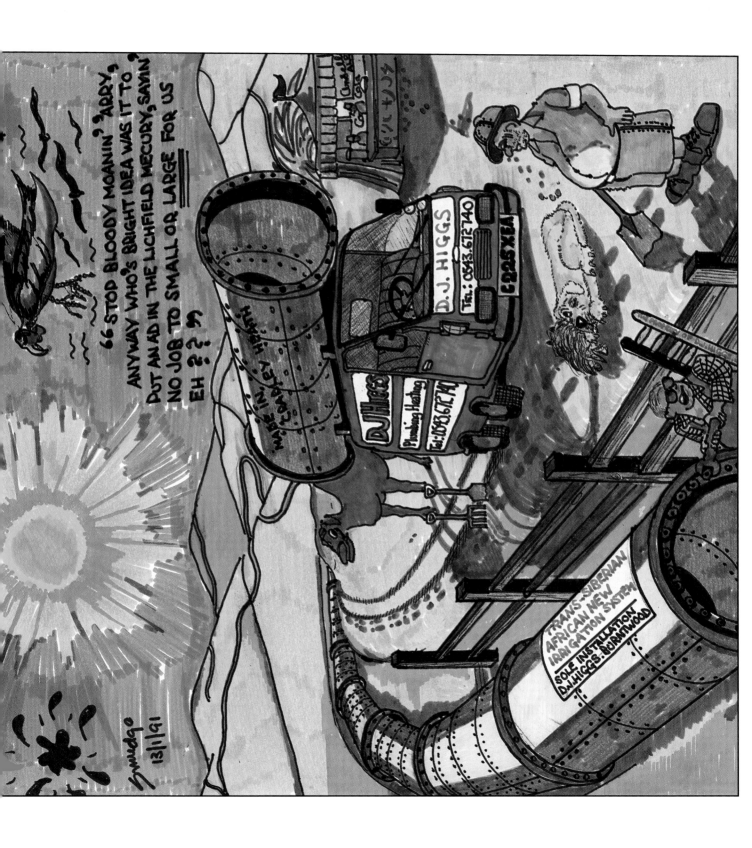

"O' DUNNO WA'S SA MARRA WI' 'IM ALL OV A SUDDEN. 'E'S ON'Y BIN THRESHIN ABOUT OUT THAYA IN THE BACK SINCE 'E 'EARD THE QUEENS GID 'ER GARDNA A MEDAL."

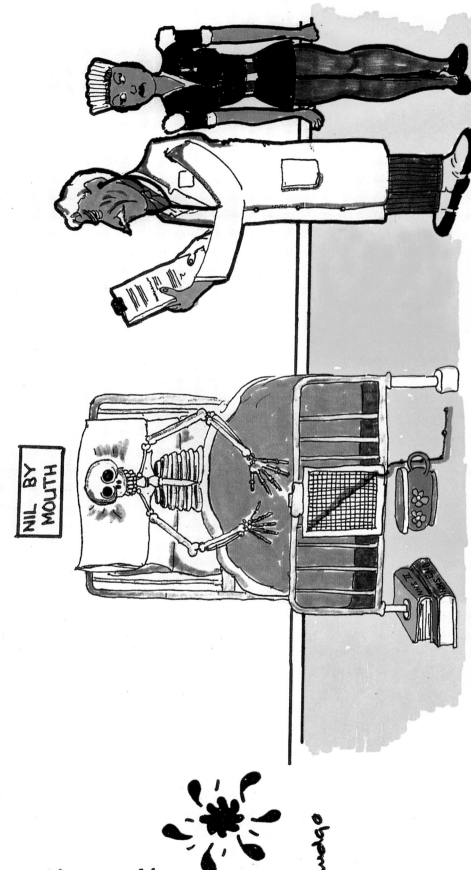

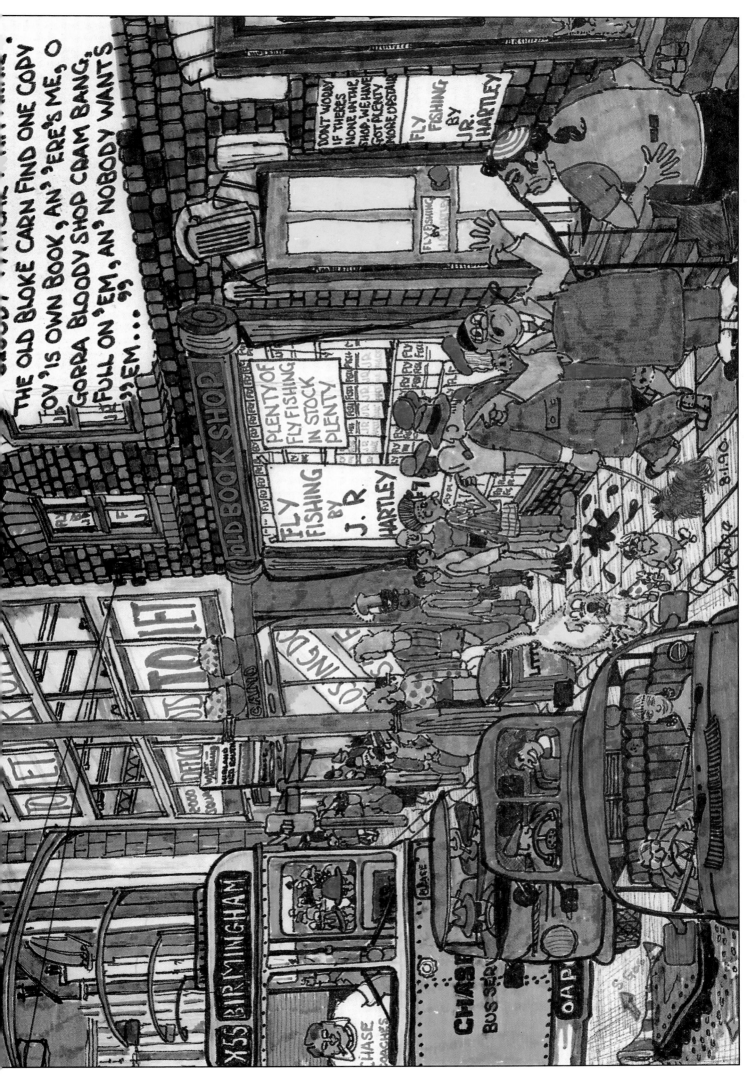

MISTA POS'MAN, MOM SEZ IS THEIR ANY CHANCE OV YO' PURRIN OWA LETTAS THROUGH
THE LETTA BOX AGEN, CUZ SHE THINKS OWA BUTCH AN'GEMMA REALLY LIKE YA' NOW!

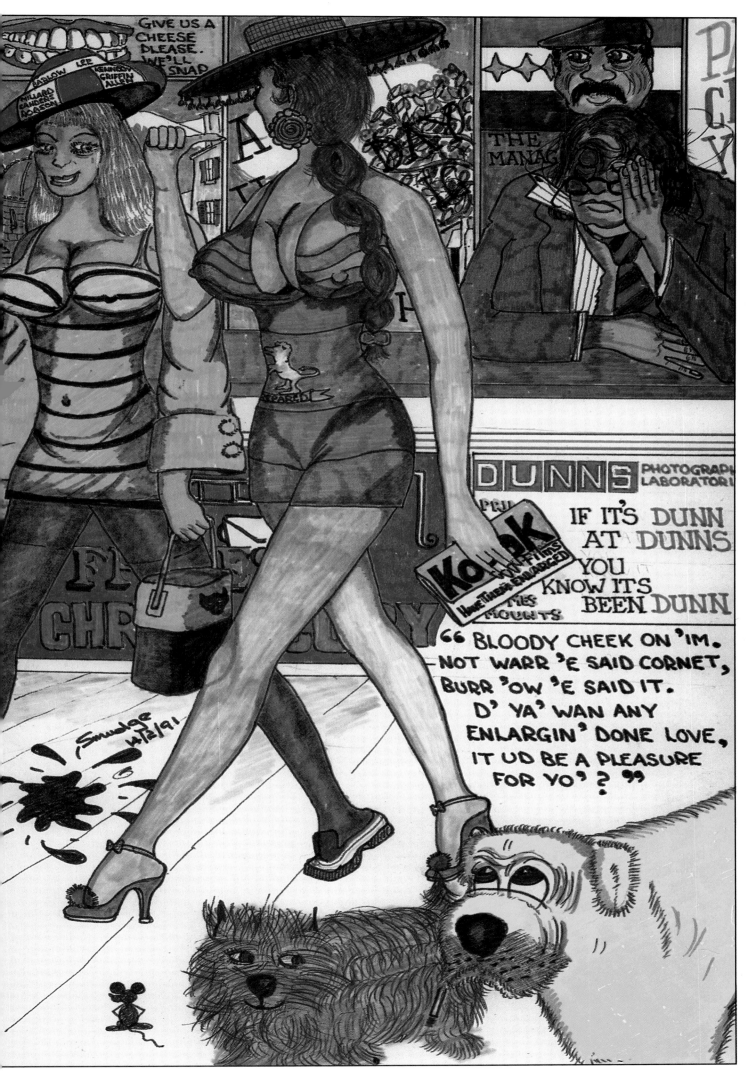

"First Annie and Jack, then, Bet and Alec, and now Vera and Jack"

"...... OF EVIDENCE IN PRIME ARE YOU AMASSING NOW MY DEAR HOLMES?"

"Not analysing, Watson, no. The Earl of Sandwell approaches, our dear houskeeper is away attending illness within her family. So I am in the process of preparing his graces favourite lunch, faggots an' gray pays."

Simons. 5/3/98

" THE GREAT ENGLISH BREAKFAST

ARTHUR . S . CURTIS   THE GREATEST PILOT IN THE WORLD EVER

To:

From:

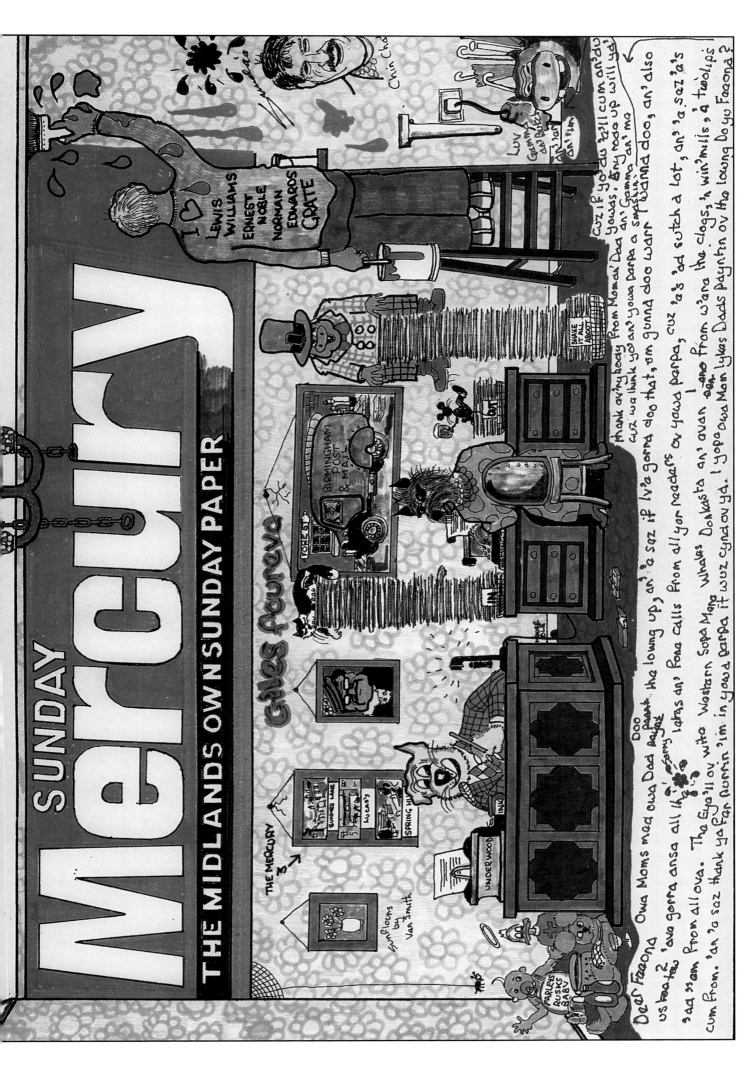

JUST A COUPLE OF BRUMMIE KIDS